NOT Such A Silent Night!

A Christmas musical for children by
Nick Perrin & Ruth Kenward
(arr. Mark Dickman)

D1872162

www.starshine.co.uk

Brown Cottage, Glynleigh Road, Hankham, East Sussex, England, BN24 5BJ.
Tel: +44 (0)1323 764334 Fax: +44 (0)1323 767145
E-mail: info@starshine.co.uk

Grateful acknowledgement is due to the following schools, which took part in pre-publication trials:
Churchwood Primary, St Leonards On Sea, E. Sussex
Glory Farm School, Bicester, Oxon.
Grovelands Primary, Hailsham, E. Sussex
Hawkes Farm Primary, Hailsham, E. Sussex
Little Ridge Primary, St Leonards on Sea, E. Sussex
Monton Green Primary, Eccles, Manchester
Park Mead Primary, Upper Dicker, E. Sussex
Rookwood Primary, Andover, Hants.
St Giles Primary Willenhall, West Midlands
Willingdon Primary, Willingdon, Eastbourne

ISBN Nos.
Musical Book: 978-1-907395-12-3
Multimedia pack: 978-1-907395-13-0

© 2011 Starshine Music Ltd.
No part of this publication may be reproduced or recorded without prior permission from Starshine Music.
The data section of the Enhanced CD contains printable resources: narrative version, pupil script/lyrics, read aloud story, programme template and PowerPoint presentation information for the sole use of the purchaser.

Cover illustration by Rachel Cloyne

© = COPY

Director's Notes

CAST LIST

Bethlehem Narrator	May be shared between two speakers.
Lamb Narrator	May be shared between two speakers.
Innkeeper	Simple speaking part.
Mary & Joseph	Simple speaking parts.
Larry Lamb	Central character, involved in the action virtually throughout, but with simple repeated lines.
Cheeky Donkey	Simple speaking part.
Mother Sheep	Simple speaking part.
Jack (Baby Donkey)	Simple speaking part.
Lucky (Baby Sheepdog)	Simple speaking part.
Sam (Baby Camel)	Simple speaking part.
Mother Donkey	Non-speaking part.
Mother Sheepdog	Non-speaking part.
Mother Camel	Non-speaking part.
Shepherds 1,2,3	Small speaking parts.
Three Wise Men	Small speaking parts.
Angels	One spoken line as a group.
Chorus	As many as are available, dressed as animals (horses, donkeys, cows, sheep, camels) and extra angels.

COSTUMES

Conventional nativity outfits, and black and white costumes for Lucky & Mother Sheepdog.

PROPS

Large sign: 'Lost'. Manger for stable, hay bales if available. Stool or small chair for Mary. Toy lamb for Shepherds to give Mary. Crooks for Shepherds (optional). Gold, frankincense and myrrh for Three Wise Men. Optional: star above the stable could be a star shaped helium balloon which is released at the end of the song 'Silent Night'.

SUGGESTED STAGE LAYOUT

Narrators are positioned as shown below. The cast sit on benches to stage left, with nativity characters, (Mary, Joseph, Innkeeper, Shepherds, Wise Men, Angels) on back rows and animals (Larry Lamb, Cheeky Donkey, Mother Sheep, Baby animals, Mother animals and Chorus) on front rows, Mother Sheep as far away as possible from the 'Lost' area. To Stage Left (or among the audience) is a <u>separated</u> area with a large sign: 'Lost', where Larry Lamb will be for most of the play.

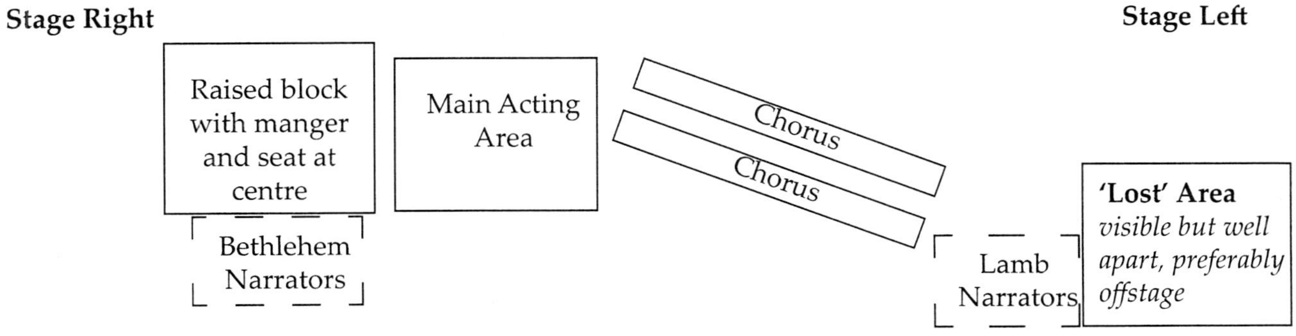

Director's Overview

INCIDENTAL	*SILENT NIGHT*	⊙ **Track 1 / 17**

It's a cold night in Bethlehem. The Innkeeper calls the animals into the stable.

SONG	**NIGHT IS COMING**	⊙ **Track 2 / 18**

The animals make such a noise that Larry Lamb is scared and runs away, though his mum told him to stay with her. The Innkeeper brings Mary and Joseph and their donkey into the stable, because all the inns are full and Mary is about to have a baby. Meanwhile, Larry Lamb is lost and all alone...

SONG	**POOR LITTLE LAMB**	⊙ **Track 3 / 19**

... until along comes a baby donkey called Jack.

SONG	**I'M A BABY DONKEY**	⊙ **Track 4 / 20**

Jack is doing what his mum told him to do, following a star. He can't help Larry to go home – he doesn't know where Larry lives. Jack continues his journey...

INCIDENTAL	*TRAVELLING MUSIC*	⊙ **Track 5 / 21**

... and is happy to be reunited with his mum at the stable. All bounce for joy!

INCIDENTAL	*BOUNCY MUSIC*	⊙ **Track 6 / 22**

Mary has had a special baby called Jesus. It's all happening at the stable, but Larry is still lost and all alone... until along comes a sheepdog pup called Lucky.

SONG	**HERE COMES A PUPPY**	⊙ **Track 7 / 23**

Lucky is doing what his mum told him, he's following a star. He can't help Larry Lamb either. Lucky continues his journey...

INCIDENTAL	*TRAVELLING MUSIC*	⊙ **Track 8 / 24**

... and is happy to be reunited with his mum at the stable. All bounce for joy!

INCIDENTAL	*BOUNCY MUSIC*	⊙ **Track 9 / 25**

But Larry is still lost and all alone... until along comes Sam the Baby Camel.

SONG	**I'M A BABY CAMEL**	⊙ **Track 10 / 26**

Sam the Camel is doing what his mum told him, he's following a star. He can't help Larry either. Sam continues his journey...

INCIDENTAL	*TRAVELLING MUSIC*	⊙ **Track 11 / 27**

... and is happy to be reunited with his mum at the stable. It's all still happening at the stable – and again all bounce for joy!

INCIDENTAL	*BOUNCY MUSIC*	⊙ **Track 12 / 28**

Meanwhile Larry Lamb is still lost and alone... until some angels arrive to guide him home.

INCIDENTAL	*SILENT NIGHT*	⊙ **Track 13 / 29**

Larry and Mother Sheep are overjoyed to be reunited with each other! Larry is also reunited with Jack, Lucky and Sam. All bounce for joy!

INCIDENTAL	*BOUNCY MUSIC (longer)*	⊙ **Track 14 / 30**

Mother Sheep leads Larry Lamb to the manger, where he meets baby Jesus.

SONG	**SILENT NIGHT**	⊙ **Track 15 / 31**

Everyone celebrates noisily. It's not such a silent night after all!

SONG	**LET'S MAKE A NOISE!**	⊙ **Track 16 / 32**

Please remember that all performances must be by prior arrangement with the Publishers from whom licences must be obtained.

NOT Such A Silent Night!

by Nick Perrin & Ruth Kenward

[ANIMALS are offstage. Nativity cast in position on benches apart from MARY, JOSEPH, MOTHER DONKEY, JACK, LUCKY & SAM, who are offstage.]

SILENT NIGHT (Incidental) **(⊙ Track 1 / 17)**

[ALL put fingers to lips and sway very gently in time to the music. Towards the end of the track fade music so that BETHLEHEM NARRATOR 1 can speak with gentle music under.]

BETH. NARR. 1 It's a cold, silent night in Bethlehem.
All is calm. All is bright.

[INNKEEPER moves onto the stage block, hand to brow as if looking for his animals.]

BETH. NARR. 2 *(pointing)* Look! The innkeeper is calling his animals into the stable. It won't be quiet for long!

NIGHT IS COMING **(⊙ Track 2 / 18)**

[CHORUS stand. INNKEEPER beckons ANIMALS ad lib, who enter as the song is sung and go to positions on benches.]

All NIGHT IS COMING.
CALL THE ANIMALS:
THEY MUST GET INDOORS!
NIGHT IS COMING.
CALL THE ANIMALS:
THEY MUST GET INDOORS!
CALL THE HORSES IN!
Horses NEIGH!
All CALL THE DONKEYS TOO!
Donkeys EE-ORE!
All CALL THE SHEEP,
CALL THE LAMBS,
CALL THE COWS IN TOO!
Cows MOO!

All NIGHT IS COMING... *(etc. as before)*

INNKEEPER:
beckoning gestures ad lib.
CHORUS:
beckoning gestures on 'call'

ANIMALS wave both hands as they make their own sounds

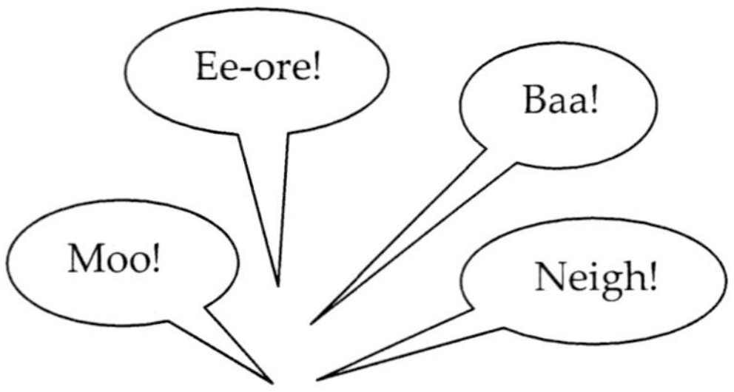

[ANIMALS make their noises simultaneously as they sit. When all are sitting, LARRY LAMB moves to Downstage Centre.]

LARRY LAMB *(shouting, with hands to ears)* It's too noisy in here!

[ANIMALS continue making noises. LARRY LAMB runs to 'Lost' area, where he keeps running on the spot.]

BETH. NARR. 1 & 2 *(shouting loudly)* Be quiet!

[ANIMALS suddenly stop making noises.]

CHEEKY DONKEY *(shoulders shaking)* Hee, hee, hee - Eee-ore!

ALL *(fingers on lips)* Ssh!

[LARRY LAMB is still running on the spot.]

MOTHER SHEEP *(in a panic)* Baa! My lamb's gone! Where is he?

[As NARRATOR speaks, MOTHER SHEEP runs round the stage searching, then runs to stand by INNKEEPER.]

LAMB NARR. 1 Larry Lamb has run away. He's scared by the noise. *(points)* Look! He's running and running, as fast as his legs will carry him!

LARRY LAMB Baa! Baa! *(stops running, stands panting.)*

LAMB NARR. 2 Larry's happy to have got away from all that noise, but he's run too far! He's lost!

LARRY LAMB *(loudly)* I'm lost! *(rubbing eyes)* Baa!

ALL *(wagging fingers)* He should have stayed with his mummy!

[LARRY sits down and rubs eyes as if crying.]

BETH. NARR. 1 Meanwhile, back at the stable, his mummy is very worried.

MOTHER SHEEP *(rubbing eyes)* Baa! I told him to stay with me!

INNKEEPER Don't worry. He'll come back.

[MOTHER SHEEP joins SHEPHERDS. ***Knocking sound.****]*

BETH. NARR. 1 Who's that knocking at the door?

[INNKEEPER steps off block to greet MARY, JOSEPH & MOTHER DONKEY as they enter Stage Right.]

It's Mary and Joseph, and Mary is about to have a baby!

BETH. NARR. 2 They can't find a place to stay because all the inns are full. But *(pointing)* that innkeeper has a stable.

INNKEEPER	You can stay in my stable.
MARY & JOSEPH	*(to INNKEEPER)* Thank you!

[INNKEEPER goes to sit with chorus. MARY sits on stool next to the manger, JOSEPH & MOTHER DONKEY stand each side.]

LAMB NARR. 1	Meanwhile, Larry Lamb is lost and all alone.
LARRY LAMB	*(rubbing eyes)* Baa! I'm lost.

POOR LITTLE LAMB (⊙ Track 3 / 19)

Clasp hands together	POOR LITTLE LAMB, POOR LITTLE LAMB. LOST AND ALL ALONE.
Wag finger in time	POOR LITTLE LAMB, POOR LITTLE LAMB. SHOULD HAVE STAYED AT HOME.

LAMB NARR. 2	Poor little lamb... But look! *(points)* Who's this coming along?
LAMB NARR. 1	It's a baby donkey!

[Enter JACK, Stage Right, sets off immediately on journey round the hall to finish with LARRY LAMB by the end of the song. N.B. JACK should not cross the stage in front of the nativity scene. CHORUS stand.]

I'M A BABY DONKEY (⊙ Track 4 / 20)

Jack	I'M A BABY DONKEY, PEOPLE CALL ME JACK. WHEN I'M BIG AND STRONG YOU RIDE UPON MY BACK.	 Flex biceps! Point to back
Chorus	HE'S A BABY DONKEY FOLLOWING A STAR. TROTTING ALONG, SINGING A SONG. EE-ORE! TROTTING ALONG, SINGING A SONG. *(loudly)* EE-ORE!	 Point upward Chorus pump arms in time; on 'Ee-ore' raise and then lower hands
	HE'S A BABY DONKEY, PEOPLE CALL HIM JACK. WHEN HE'S BIG AND STRONG YOU RIDE UPON HIS BACK HE'S A BABY DONKEY... *(etc., as before)*	Actions as above

[CHORUS sit. JACK arrives by LARRY LAMB.]

LAMB NARR. 1	Jack's mum carried Mary all the way to Bethlehem. Now he's following a star to find her.
JACK	*(points)* I'm following that star because my mum told me to.
LARRY LAMB	That's nice, but I'm lost. *(rubbing eyes)* Baa!
ALL	*(wagging fingers)* He should have stayed with his mummy!

LAMB NARR. 2	Jack would like to help Larry find his way home, but he doesn't know where he lives.
JACK	I'm <u>really</u> sorry, but I don't know where you live. *(waving)* Bye.

[JACK travels to stand Downstage, facing the manger.]

<u>TRAVELLING MUSIC</u> (Incidental) (⊙ Track 5 / 21)

BETH. NARR. 1	Guess where Jack has found his mum?
ALL	In the stable!
JACK	*(loudly, pointing)* There's my mum! *(waves)*

[MOTHER DONKEY runs to hug JACK, D/stage Centre and they dance round in a circle. CHORUS bounce where they are.]

<u>BOUNCY MUSIC</u> (Incidental) (⊙ Track 6 / 22)

ALL	*(flinging arms up)* Hooray!
MARY JOSEPH INNKEEPER	Ssh! Don't wake the baby!
ALL	*(stage whisper)* Sorry!

[JACK & MOTHER DONKEY sit by MARY as NARR. speaks.]

BETH. NARR. 2	Mary's had a baby called Jesus. He's a very special baby.
LAMB NARR. 1	It's all happening in the stable, but Larry is still lost and alone.
LARRY LAMB	*(rubs eyes)* Baa!
LAMB NARR. 2	Poor little lamb. But look! *(points)* Who's this coming along?
LAMB NARR. 1	It's a puppy!

[Enter LUCKY, Stage R., sets off immediately on journey round the hall to finish by LARRY LAMB at the end of the song. N.B. Avoid crossing in front of the nativity scene. CHORUS stand.]

<u>HERE COMES A PUPPY</u> (⊙ Track 7 / 23)

Chorus

HERE COMES A PUPPY! LUCKY THE SHEEPDOG PUP! BOUNCING! TAIL WAGGING! LUCKY THE SHEEPDOG PUP!	Move up and down on the spot, with a slight bounce
JUST GIVE A WHISTLE! ← *(mime whistling for a bar!)*	ALL stand still... then mime whistling
JUST GIVE A WHISTLE! HE WILL SOON BE THERE. ←	LARRY LAMB beckons LUCKY, who bounds up to him

Lucky	I AM A PUPPY LUCKY THE SHEEPDOG PUP BOUNCING! TAIL WAGGING! LUCKY THE SHEEPDOG PUP	As before
Chorus	JUST GIVE A WHISTLE… *(etc.)*	

… *(at the very end)* Woof, woof!

[CHORUS sit. LUCKY arrives by LARRY LAMB.]

LAMB NARR. 1 — Lucky's mum is a sheepdog. She's been helping some shepherds take their sheep to Bethlehem. Now Lucky is following a star to find her.

LUCKY — *(points)* I'm following that star because my mum told me to.

LARRY LAMB — That's nice, but I'm lost. *(rubbing eyes)* Baa!

ALL — *(wagging fingers)* He should have stayed with his mummy!

LAMB NARR. 2 — Lucky would like to help Larry find his way home, but he doesn't know where he lives.

LUCKY — I'm <u>really</u> sorry, but I don't know where you live. *(waving)* Bye.

[Exit LUCKY. Enter SHEPHERDS & MOTHER SHEEP-DOG, to approach Stable area.]

<u>TRAVELLING MUSIC</u> (Incidental) (⊙ Track 8 / 24)

SHEPHERD 1 — We have come to see the baby King.

SHEPHERD 2 — The angels told us how to find you.

SHEPHERD 3 — *(giving lamb to MARY)* We have brought you this gift.

[SHEPHERDS kneel by manger. LUCKY enters.]

BETH. NARR. 1 — Guess where Lucky has found <u>his</u> mum?

ALL — In the stable!

LUCKY — *(loudly, pointing)* There's my mum! *(waves)*

[MOTHER SHEEPDOG & LUCKY run to hug D/stage Centre and dance in a circle. CHORUS bounce where they are.]

<u>BOUNCY MUSIC</u> (Incidental) (⊙ Track 9 / 25)

ALL — *(flinging arms up)* Hooray!

ALL IN STABLE — Ssh! Don't wake the baby!

[LUCKY & MOTHER SHEEPDOG go to sit by MARY as NARRATOR speaks.]

LAMB NARR. 1 — It's all happening in the stable, but Larry is still lost and alone.

LARRY LAMB	*(rubs eyes)* Baa!
LAMB NARR. 2	Poor little lamb. But look! *(points)* Who's this coming along?
ALL	It's a baby camel!

[Enter SAM Stage Right, sets off immediately on journey round the hall to finish by LARRY LAMB at the end of the song. N.B. Avoid crossing in front of the nativity scene. CHORUS stand.]

I'M A BABY CAMEL (⊙ Track 10 / 26)

Sam

I'M A BABY CAMEL.
ONLY GOT ONE HUMP.
I'M A DROMEDARY:
JUST THE ONE HUMP. ← Hold out index finger

Chorus

CAMELS IN THE DESERT
MOSTLY HAVE TWO HUMPS.
SAM'S A DROMEDARY:
JUST THE ONE HUMP! — As before

[ALL those standing do a slow turn on the spot with hands over head, palms together, or doing 'sand dance' hand moves.]

CAMELS IN THE DESERT
MOSTLY HAVE TWO HUMPS.
SAM'S A DROMEDARY:
JUST THE ONE HUMP! — As before

[ALL finish with hands over head palms together. SAM arrives by LARRY LAMB. CHORUS sit.]

LAMB NARR. 1	Sam's mother carried one of the Three Wise Men all the way from the East. Now Sam is following a star to find her.
SAM	*(points)* I'm following that star because my mum told me to.
LARRY LAMB	That's nice, but I'm still lost! *(rubbing eyes)* Baa!
ALL	*(wagging fingers)* He should have stayed with his mummy!
LAMB NARR. 2	Sam would like to help Larry find his way home, but he doesn't know where Larry lives.
SAM	I'm <u>really</u> sorry, but I don't know where you live. *(waving)* Bye.

[Exit SAM. WISE MEN & MOTHER CAMEL go to place gifts by manger.]

TRAVELLING MUSIC (Incidental) (⊙ Track 11 / 27)

WISE MAN 1	We have come to see the baby King.
WISE MAN 2	We've been following a star to find you.
WISE MAN 3	We have brought gifts.

WISE MAN 1 *(giving it)* Gold!

WISE MAN 2 *(giving it)* Frankincense!

WISE MAN 3 *(giving it)* Myrrh!

[WISE MEN stand behind manger. Enter SAM.]

BETH. NARR. 1 Guess where Sam has found <u>his</u> mum?

ALL In the stable!

SAM *(loudly, pointing at MOTHER CAMEL)* There's my mum! *(waves)*

[MOTHER CAMEL runs to hug SAM D/stage Centre and they dance round in a circle. CHORUS bounce where they are.]

<u>BOUNCY MUSIC</u> (Incidental) (⊙ Track 12 / 28)

ALL *(flinging arms up)* Hooray!

ALL IN STABLE Ssh! Don't wake the baby!

[SAM & MOTHER CAMEL go to sit by MARY as NARRATOR speaks.]

LAMB NARR. 2 It's all happening in the stable, but Larry Lamb is still lost and alone.

LARRY LAMB *(rubs eyes)* Baa!

LAMB NARR. 1 Poor little lamb. But look! *(points)* Who's this coming along?

[ANGELS stand, and begin to move towards 'Lost' area.]

LAMB NARR. 1 It's the angels!

LAMB NARR. 2 The angels know where little lamb lives. They will take him home.

ANGELS *(beckoning)* Cheer up, little lamb! We'll take you home!

[ANGELS move each side of LARRY LAMB. During the music they lead LARRY LAMB among the audience and back to the stage – not taking too lengthy a route; then return to places leaving LARRY LAMB facing the manger. Fade music when ready.]

<u>SILENT NIGHT</u> (Incidental) (⊙ Track 13 / 29)

BETH. NARR. 1 Guess where Larry Lamb lives?

ALL In the stable!

BETH. NARR. 1 And he's found his mum at last!

LARRY LAMB *(waving at MOTHER SHEEP)* There's my mum!

ALL — *(clapping)* He's back with his mummy!

[MOTHER SHEEP runs to hug LARRY LAMB D/stage Centre and they dance round in a circle. CHORUS bounce where they are - cheering on the last bar of the music.]

<u>BOUNCY MUSIC (Longer)</u> (Incid.) **(⦿ Track 14 / 30)**

ALL ANIMALS — *(flinging arms up)* Hooray!

ALL HUMANS — Ssh! Don't wake the baby!

MOTHER SHEEP — Look, Larry! It's baby Jesus!

BETH. NARR. 1 — Mother Sheep is taking Larry to see baby Jesus.

[MOTHER SHEEP leads LARRY LAMB to the manger, where he kneels down. MARY picks up baby Jesus and cradles him in her arms. JACK, LUCKY & SAM go to stand near the manger too.]

BETH. NARR. 2 — Now it's very peaceful in the stable.

<u>SILENT NIGHT</u> **(⦿ Track 15 / 31)**

> Could be sung by a small group

> N.B. the last three notes of this wide ranging melody have been adapted to suit infant voices

SILENT NIGHT, HOLY NIGHT.
ALL IS CALM, ALL IS BRIGHT
ROUND THE VIRGIN MOTHER AND CHILD.
HOLY INFANT SO TENDER AND MILD,
SLEEP IN HEAVENLY PEACE.
SLEEP IN HEAVENLY PEACE.

JACK
LUCKY
SAM
LARRY LAMB — *(very loudly)* What a lovely baby!

ALL — Ssh! He's asleep!

CHEEKY DONKEY — *(shoulders shaking)* Hee, hee, hee! He's not asleep any more! Eee-ore!

LARRY LAMB — *(loudly)* Great! Now we can celebrate!

ALL — Hooray!

ALL NARRATORS — It's <u>not</u> such a silent night after all!

[EVERYONE stands, all ANIMALS making their noises as they do so. Children might play along with instruments during the song, or play kazoos during 2nd time through.]

LET'S MAKE A NOISE!

(⊙ Track 16 / 32)

Clap in time

LET'S MAKE A NOISE!
LET'S MAKE A NOISE!
NOW IT'S CHRISTMAS DAY!
LET'S MAKE A NOISE!
LET'S MAKE A NOISE!
JESUS BORN TODAY!

Clap three times

Jump → JUMPING FOR JOY 'COS WE FEEL DELIGHT!
Shake heads → THAT'S WHY IT'S NOT SUCH A SILENT NIGHT!

JUMPING FOR JOY 'COS WE FEEL DELIGHT!
THAT'S WHY IT'S NOT SUCH A SILENT NIGHT!

As before

MAKE LOTS OF NOISE!
MAKE LOTS OF NOISE!
MAKE LOTS OF NOISE TONIGHT!
ALL RIGHT!

Clap in time

(repeat)

(shout) HOORAY!

STARSHINE Music
© 2011 Starshine Music Ltd.
Tel: +44 (0)1323 764334 Fax: +44 (0)1323 767145
Website: www.starshine.co.uk e-mail: info@starshine.co.uk

Please remember that all performances must be by prior arrangement with the Publishers from whom licences must be obtained.

PowerPoint Presentation
LYRICS for Data Projection

Easily create your own song words database for use with projection software and computers

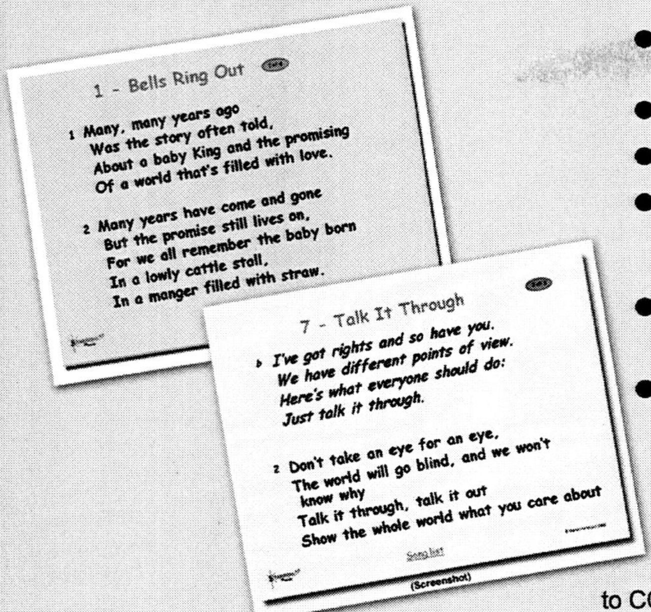

- Powerpoint Presentation for use with Data Projectors, PC's and interactive whiteboards.
- Lyrics clearly laid out.
- Quick links to all songs.
- Licensed for use on all individual school/church computers once registered on your CCLI report or a Starshine Repro Licence has been purchased.
- Available for each of our products when the Book & CD are purchased.
- Please ensure your annual CCLI report is completed and returned.

The PPT presentation is

FREE

to CCLI licence holders. For organisations without a CCLI licence, a Starshine Repro Licence can be purchased for a small fee.

To obtain the PowerPoint presentation:-

CCLI Licence holders - email: **info@starshine.co.uk** stating your organisation's name, post code, invoice number of the product purchased, product name and your CCLI number. Once verified, the presentation will be emailed to you.

For non CCLI Licence holders - telephone Starshine Music on 01323 764334 to purchase a Starshine Repro Licence.

All our children's songs are available as downloads from:

iTunes

Track1 & 17 (incid.)
Track 13 (demo)
Track 29 (backing)

Silent Night

For Incidental purposes play from bar 5

Trad, arr. Mark Dickman

© 2011 Starshine Music Ltd.
All rights reserved.

D♭
A♭
E♭
E♭7
Ho - ly in - fant so ten - der and mild, sleep in hea - ven - ly
11
A♭
A♭/E♭
E♭7
A♭
pea - ce. Sleep_ in hea - ven-ly peace.
14

Track 2 (demo)
Track 18 (backing)

Night Is Coming

N. Perrin & R. Kenward
(arr. M. Dickman)

Steadily (♩ = 74)

© 2011 Starshine Music Ltd.
All rights reserved.

Em7(♭5) A+ A Dm C F
They must get in - doors! Call the hor - ses in! Neigh!
11
C F Em7(♭5) A7 Em7(♭5) A7
Call the don - keys too! Ee - ore! Call the sheep! Call the lambs!
15
1. 2.
N.C. Dm Dm
Call the cows in too! Moo! too! Moo!
19

Poor Little Lamb

N. Perrin & R. Kenward
(arr. M. Dickman)

Adagio (♩. = 45)

© 2011 Starshine Music Ltd.
All rights reserved.

Track 4 (demo)
Track 20 (backing)

I'm A Baby Donkey

N. Perrin & R. Kenward
(arr. M. Dickman)

© 2011 Starshine Music Ltd.
All rights reserved.

A E B7 E
All He's a ba - by don - key foll - ow - ing a star,
13
A B E
trot - ting a - long, sing - ing a song. Ee - ore!
17
A B E N.C. E
trot - ting a - long, sing - ing a song. Ee - ore!
21

Track 5, 8, 11 (demo)
Track 21, 24, 27 (backing)

Travelling Music

N. Perrin & R. Kenward
(arr. M. Dickman)

© 2011 Starshine Music Ltd.
All rights reserved.

Track 6/9/12 (demo)
Track 22/25/28 (backing)
Longer version: Track 14/30

Bouncy Music

N. Perrin & R. Kenward
(arr. M. Dickman)

Steady (♩. = 130)

© 2011 Starshine Music Ltd.
All rights reserved.

Track 7 (demo)
Track 23 (backing)

Here Comes A Puppy

N. Perrin & R. Kenward
(arr. M. Dickman)

Lively 2 beat (♩ = 175)

© 2011 Starshine Music Ltd.
All rights reserved.

G D G D
All Just give a whistle (whistle)
13
1.
G D A7 D
Just give a whis - tle! He will soon be there.
17
2.
D G D Bm Em7 A7 D
there.
21

Track 10 (demo)
Track 26 (backing)

I'm A Baby Camel

N. Perrin & R. Kenward
(arr. M. Dickman)

Funky camel! (♩ = 160)

© 2011 Starshine Music Ltd.
All rights reserved.

2.
Em D Em
15
D Em D F♯m7(♭5) B7 Em
18
Em D Em D Em
Cam - els in the des - ert most - ly have two humps. Sam's a dro - me -
23
D F♯m7(♭5) B Em N.C. Em
- da - ry: just the one hump.
28

Track 16 (demo)
Track 32 (backing)

Let's Make A Noise

N. Perrin & R. Kenward
(arr. M. Dickman)

Bright (♩ = 150)

© 2011 Starshine Music Ltd.
All rights reserved.

F C/E G/D C F C/E Dm7 G6 C
Jump - ing for joy 'cos we feel de - light! That's why it's NOT such a si - lent night!
(jump)
(clap, clap, clap)
(shake heads)
13
F C/E G/D C F C/E Dm7 G6 C
Jump - ing for joy 'cos we feel de - light! That's why it's NOT such a si - lent night!
(jump)
(clap, clap, clap)
(shake heads)
17
G+ C/G G+ C/G Dm7 G7
1.
C
Make lots of noise! Make lots of noise! Make lots of noise to - night! All right!
Clap every beat to end.
21
2.
C Dm7 G7 C
night! All right!
Hoo- ray!
25

Copyright & Licensing – General Information

WHY LICENCES?

Royalties collected from performing and copyright licences are the main source of income for writers. It is a publisher's duty to collect royalties on the writer's behalf. **Intellectual copyright is protected by law.** When copyright is not respected and royalties are not paid, writers are deprived of income and there is little or no incentive for writers to produce new materials.

WHICH ACTIVITIES REQUIRE LICENCES?

Performing our musicals (including songs from the musicals)	All musicals are protected by 'Grand Rights'. If you are planning to stage a 'Starshine' musical (in whole or in part) you will need to apply direct to Starshine Music for a **PERFORMING LICENCE**. 'Block' licences which your school/group/LEA may have do not cover performances of musicals.
Recording our musicals and songs (video, DVD, sound)	You must apply direct to Starshine Music for a **RECORDING LICENCE.**
Copying songs from our songbooks (Assembly & Concert Collection)	If you photocopy or reproduce our music and/or lyrics to create song sheets or OHPs (or copy or store music/lyrics on computer), a licence is required. • If your organisation is covered by a licence issued by **CCLI** (Schools: CWCL, CWMRL; Churches: CCL, MRL), then it is necessary to list the songs you copy/ reproduce on their Copy Report. Please ensure the annual return is sent to CCLI. • If your organisation is not covered by CCLI then you need to apply direct to Starshine Music for a **STARSHINE REPRO LICENCE.**
Performing songs from our songbooks (Assembly & Concert Collection)	• If your organisation has an arrangement with the **Performing Rights Society (PRS)** either directly or through an LEA, public performance of songs should be declared to PRS. • If your organisation does not have an arrangement with the PRS and wishes to perform our songs in public, please apply direct to Starshine Music for a **STARSHINE PERFORMING LICENCE.**

APPLYING FOR A LICENCE FROM STARSHINE MUSIC

- **Online** – *by completing the form on our website (or you may print the form and send or fax it to us).*
- **Application form** – *available in the director's book. Copy, then post or fax it to us.*
- **Telephone** - *and we can talk you through the process.*

APPLYING FOR A CCLI LICENCE

- **UK** - tel 01323 436103. For countries **outside the UK** see – www.ccli.com

MORE INFORMATION ON LICENSING & COPYRIGHT

Detailed information and links to all the major copyright agencies, including **'A Guide to Copyright in Schools'** can be found on our website.

Starshine Music Tel – **01323 764334** Fax – **01323 767145** **www.starshine.co.uk**

PERFORMING RIGHTS FOR THE SHOW

LICENCE APPLICATION

If you are planning to stage this musical, or to record the performance and/or songs, you will need to apply for a Licence. 'Block' licences which your school/group may have do **not** cover performances of musicals, licences for which are only available directly from publishers. To perform any musical without a specific licence to do so from its publisher is illegal.

Revenue raised from Performing Licences is the main source of income for writers. Licence charges vary according to publishers and performing circumstances, but our licence fees are very reasonable and safeguard you from prosecution. A quotation for your proposed production may be obtained from Starshine Music by phone / e-mail / website. Alternatively, you may complete the form below, and post or fax it to:

Starshine Music Ltd., Brown Cottage, Glynleigh Rd, Hankham, E. Sussex, England. BN24 5BJ.
Tel: 0844 846 4812 Fax: 0844 846 9053 (Overseas Tel: +44 1323 764334 Fax: +44 1323 767145)
Website: www.starshine.co.uk

Please give me a price quotation ☐ **Please process this application** ☐

APPLICATION TO PERFORM:

'Not Such A Silent Night' by Nick Perrin & Ruth Kenward

Name of school / group ....

Date(s) of production ....

Venue ....

Number of performances (excluding Dress Rehearsal to school) ....

Expected audience size per performance ....

Will admissions be charged (& if so, at what rate)? ....

Will voluntary contributions be collected? ....

Contact name ....

Address of school / group ....

....

.... Postcode ....

Daytime telephone number .... Fax: ....

e-mail address ....

If you are intending to record the show, or any part of it, please estimate the number of copies you will be producing. (Include an approximate figure to cover parents making DVD/video recordings, as well as any 'official' school recordings.)

DVD/VIDEO RECORDING	1-5	6-25	26-50	51-75	76-100	☐	(est. no. if over 100)
SOUND RECORDING	1-5	6-25	26-50	51-75	76-100	☐	

Index of Musical Items

Title		CD Demos	CD Backings	Script Page	Score Page
Silent Night	*(incid.)*	1	17	5	15
Night Is Coming		2	18	5	17
Poor Little Lamb		3	19	7	19
I'm A Baby Donkey		4	20	7	20
Travelling Music	*(incid.)*	5	21	8	22
Bouncy Music	*(incid.)*	6	22	8	23
Here Comes A Puppy		7	23	8	24
Travelling Music	*(incid.)*	8	24	9	22
Bouncy Music	*(incid.)*	9	25	9	23
I'm A Baby Camel		10	26	10	26
Travelling Music	*(incid.)*	11	27	10	22
Bouncy Music	*(incid.)*	12	28	11	23
Silent Night	*(incid.)*	13	29	11	15
Bouncy Music (longer)	*(incid.)*	14	30	12	23
Silent Night		15	31	12	15
Let's Make A Noise!		16	32	13	28

View detailed information about all our products and listen to samples of all our songs at:

www.starshine.co.uk